Knit & Stitch
for beginners

Knit & Stitch
for beginners

Wendy Freeman

BARRON'S

First edition for North America published in 2005
by Barron's Educational Series, Inc.
First published by MQ Publications Limited, 2005
Copyright © 2005 MQ Publications Limited
Text copyright © 2005 Wendy Freeman

MQ Publications Limited
12 The Ivories, 6–8 Northampton Street
London N1 2HY
www.mqpublications.com
Editor: *Katy Bevan*
Photography: *Lizzie Orme*
Illustrations: *Rachael Matthews*
Design concept: *C-B Design*

All inquiries should be addressed to:
Barron's Educational Series, Inc.
250 Wireless Boulevard
Hauppauge, New York 11788
www.barronseduc.com

This book contains the opinions and ideas of the
author. The author and publisher disclaim all
responsibility for any liability, loss, or risk, personal
or otherwise, which is incurred as a consequence,
directly or indirectly, of the use and application of
any of the contents of this book.

ISBN-13: 978-0-7641-5864-3
ISBN-10: 0-7641-5864-3

Library of Congress Catalog Card No: 2004116194

Printed and bound in China
9 8 7 6 5 4 3 2 1

Contents

Introduction

For years knitting has had the image of being old-fashioned and dull. But now with exciting new yarns available, hand knitting is big news! The advent of the celebrity knitter has certainly helped boost the handicrafts cool factor. The younger generation is joining the latest trend, cult knitting. It involves claiming those long forgotten pointed weapons—Grandma's old knitting needles. The upsurge in interest has led to some groups meeting regularly in public places and on public transportation. Knitting makes for a great urban hobby because yarn and needles are light and portable!

For all those who are into the idea of knitting and stitching but bored or intimidated by technicalities, this book provides the inspiration to pick up those needles and start knitting.

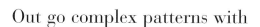

Out go complex patterns with incomprehensible instructions and complicated techniques, and in come simple patterns with quick results and clever shortcuts to save time and effort. This book enables you to create fantastic, fun, and functional fashion using minimum skills to maximum effect. In addition to the projects, which have full instructions and visual explanations, there are also suggestions for extra accessories that will bring a touch of individualism to your own work. Making unique and fun items couldn't be easier.

Don't just sit there—knit something!

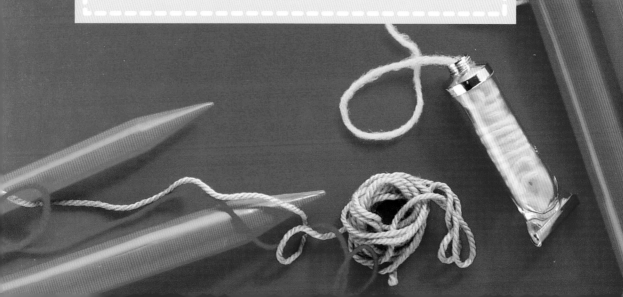

How to
Knit

Tools for Knitting

You will need the right tools for the job—make a collection of your needles and equipment and keep them together in an organized bag.

crochet hooks

KNITTING NEEDLES

These are the principal tools that you will require. They are available in various sizes and lengths and are usually bought in pairs. The length of the needle you use is down to personal preference. If you are knitting a large garment, use longer needles, but if you are only knitting a small piece, you can use shorter, less cumbersome ones.

HOMEMADE NEEDLES

If you want to knit with really chunky yarn and you can't buy needles big enough, simply make your own with dowels or broom handles available from hardware stores. Shape one end of the needle using a craft knife and then sand it down well so the yarn won't snag on it. Bind the other end with tape so that the stitches don't fall off. Knitting is a lot quicker with smooth needles so take care of them by keeping them clean. Store them in a safe place where they won't get bent.

ROW COUNTER

To keep a tally of the number of rows you have knitted, use a row counter. These are especially useful when working on more complex patterns.

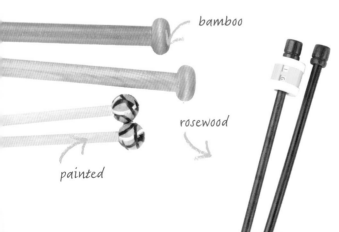

bamboo

rosewood

painted

cable needles

stitch holder

RECORDS

It is a good idea to find a way of keeping a record of what you have made—instructions, sketches, samples, and records of the needle sizes used. It is also useful to make a note of any difficulties you experience.

tape measure

stitch markers

flexible needles

needle gauge

YOU MAY ALSO NEED

✱ Sharp scissors; a tape measure; knitters sewing needles (needles that are blunt with big eyes); and crochet hooks for picking up any dropped stitches.

Other knitting paraphernalia include stitch markers to keep a track of your progress; double-pointed cable needles for decorative patterns; and stitch holders in a variety of different sizes.

Yarns

If you want to knit, the first thing you'll have to do is get yourself some yarn.

double knitting

cotton

YARN TYPES

There is an overwhelming variety of yarns on the market today. In this book I have used a selection of my favorites. Yarns are made up of different plies. A ply is a single strand, so the number of strands twisted together to make the yarn denote the ply. The twisting of yarn makes it knittable; if it was not twisted it would be weak and break. There are many unusual yarns available from glittery and whiskery to slubby and knobbly. Once a yarn has been spun it is made into balls or hanks. They are sold in varying weights and are available in craft stores, direct from mills, or on the Internet (see suppliers on page 155).

worsted weight

DYE LOTS

If you are knitting one of the larger projects and need to match several balls to the same color it is worth noting the shade and dye lot on the label. To ensure that you get exactly the same color you will need to check that these numbers match up, since different dye lots may produce slightly different shades. It is preferable to buy a little more than you need, than to run out half way through.

twisted yarn

bulky yarn

mohair

Fancy Yarns

BE A COLLECTOR

To find more unusual yarns I love delving through bargain bins in knitting yarn stores, garage sales, and flea markets. These yarns can be picked up cheaply and there is nothing better than your creations having a story behind them. I like to look back and remember where I have gotten a yarn from, like a foreign flea market find, for instance, mixed with a yarn bought in a thrift store on a Scottish island! Of course, you don't have to knit with yarn. Interesting experiments can be had with strips of fabric, ribbon, or yarn you've made yourself, such as spool knitting, plaits, or braids.

bulky chenille

cotton tape

use more than one strand

BUYING YARNS

For most of the projects in the book there is no need to use large quantities of yarn. In fact, some of the more unusual fibers can be overwhelming, and are better bought and used in smaller quantities.

Snap up discontinued or out of season yarns at reduced prices. Combine odd balls to make exciting and fresh designs in fabulous color combinations. This book will show you how to put yarns together in unexpected ways.

fine mohair

FANCY FIBERS

Some of the myriad fibers available include slubs, cotton tapes, and ribbons. Mohair is fine and fluffy and is often good mixed with other more substantial yarns. There are many yarns that come ready-mixed, which may combine natural and man-made fibers. Some of these have good longevity and will withstand washing well, so it is best to take into account the use that the garment will have. For instance, a purse may need to be more durable than a scarf.

alpaca-silk mix

Casting on: Knit method

There are many different ways of casting on. This is
perhaps one of the simplest to learn and uses both needles.

2 Insert the second needle into this
stitch, starting underneath the first
needle so that the two needles cross each
other and right needle is behind the left.
Taking the yarn in your right hand, loop it up
over the lower needle, between the needles.

1 Place a slipknot (see tip box opposite)
on the left needle, pulling the tail end
so that the loop fits the size of needle
firmly. This is your first stitch.

3 Draw the yarn through the loop to form a stitch.

New stitches will be added to your left hand needle.

4 Slip this stitch onto the left needle and pull the yarn to tighten the stitch. Insert the right needle into the second stitch and put the yarn around the end of the right needle. Draw the yarn through to form a stitch. Place the stitch on the left needle. Repeat these steps until you have the required number of stitches.

Long-tail cast on

Another method of casting on is using the
thumb; this gives a more elastic edge and some
people find it quicker to complete.

① Measure a length of yarn three times
the length of the final cast-on width.
Make a slip knot at this point and slip it onto
a needle of the correct size for your pattern.

② Wind the short end of the yarn once
around the left thumb, clockwise.
Insert the point of the right needle into
the front of the loop on the thumb.

3 Wind the long end of the yarn around the needle in a clockwise direction, and pull a loop of yarn through onto the needle.

4 Slip the loop off the thumb and tighten the yarn to form a stitch. Repeat until you have the required number of stitches.

TIP

✳ There are plenty of ways to cast on stitches, these are just two. You may choose different cast-ons for certain occasions. Find a method that suits you, and the nature of your project.

Holding the Needle

It may feel awkward trying to hold
your needles at first—expert knitters make
it look so easy—but it will soon become
second nature.

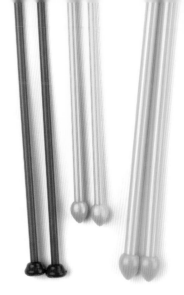

Some knitters like to hold the right
needle in the same way as a pencil, as
shown here. For casting on and working the
first few rows, the knitted piece passes over
the hand, between the thumb and index
finger. As work progresses, allow the thumb
to slide under the knitted piece.

TIP

* Some larger needles are more difficult
to hold—but the speed at which your
knitting grows makes up for any discomfort!

2 The left needle is held slightly over the top, using the thumb and index finger to control the tip of the needle. If it feels more comfortable, you can hold the right hand needle in that way as well.

Very soon you will be knitting things for yourself

3 To begin with, hold the two needles evenly, at elbow height. You will find that you develop your own style after a time. Some knitters like to hold one of the needles firmly under an arm to speed things up, and help take the weight of the knitting.

Holding the Yarn

The aim is to keep your stitches all at the same tension. With a little patience and practice you'll quickly get the hang of it.

1 It is important that you develop some method of controlling the tension on the yarn as this keeps the stitches all the same size. Start by wrapping the yarn around the little finger of your right hand.

2 Then weave the yarn through the fingers, over the third, under the second, and then over the index finger.

③ The yarn should pass over the top of the index finger so that you can use the smallest movement possible to get the yarn over your needle.

TIP

✻ This is known as the English, or right-handed way to hold the yarn. On the continent they hold the yarn in the left hand, which may be easier if you are left-handed.

✻ Keep the stitches toward the tip of the needle. This way the yarn will not be stretched between the needles.

✻ Make sure that you are sitting comfortably, so that there is no strain on your back, or neck.

④ Now you can hold the needle in your right hand. This method should keep the stitches loose and easy to work with. There are many variations on the way to hold the yarn so find whichever way suits you.

Knit

Now that you have cast on your first row, it is time to make a stitch. The knit stitch is the simplest and is worked from front to back.

① Keeping the yarn behind the right needle, insert the point of the right needle into the front of the stitch (from left to right, and front to back).

② The yarn starts at the back of the work, and passes clockwise around the back needle, and then between the two needles.

3 Draw the loop through the front of the work with the point of the right needle. This is your new stitch.

4 Slip the stitch you have just worked off the left needle. You will have formed a new stitch on the right needle.

TIP

✱ When you knit all rows, you will be making garter stitch, which has a rough bobbly texture—this smooth finish is stockinette stitch (see page 30).

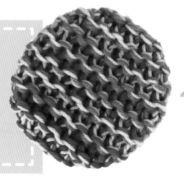

Knit a few rows to practice, then save your first sample swatches to make buttons.

Purl

This is another stitch, that in combination with the knit stitch allows you to create many new stitch patterns. Note the textured appearance of the purl stitches.

1 Keeping the yarn in front of the right needle, insert the point of the right needle through the front of the stitch (from right to left).

2 Pass the yarn over the point of the right needle from right to left, and down to the front.

3 With the point of the right needle draw the yarn through the stitch (toward the back).

4 Slip the stitch you have just worked into off the left needle. You have formed a new purl stitch on the right needle.

PURLY QUEENS

✳ Using just the knit and purl stitches you can make plenty of patterns—seed stitch uses alternate knit and purl stitches and creates a dense and bobbly fabric.

GET GOING

You are now ready to work stockinette stitch (knit one row, purl one row, and repeat). Practice a few rows. You will notice that the knit rows are smooth and the purl rows are textured. The smooth side is the "right" side and the rough side is the reverse side (see page 31).

Binding off

A bind-off row is a row that closes off the free
loops so they don't unravel. Check the bind-off
as you go along to make sure that it isn't pulling
tight or frilling because it is too loose.

 Work 2 stitches. It is easiest to do
this on a knit row.

② With the left needle pull the first stitch
over the second, and right off both of
the knitting needles.

③ Work another stitch and pull the previous one over it.

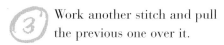

The bound off edge often shows, so keep it neat.

④ Repeat Step 3 to the end. Trim the yarn. Pull the last loop, thread the yarn through it, and pull tight.

Basic Combinations

With only knit and purl you can make all sorts of different stitches, combining the rough with the smooth—here are a few examples.

GARTER STITCH

This has a rough texture and is created by using the knit stitch on every stitch of every row. It creates a dense, tough fabric that is useful for bags and hardwearing accessories.

Stockinette stitch

Garter stitch

STOCKINETTE STITCH

This is the traditional stitch used for most jersey fabric, and one that most people will be familiar with. It is created by knitting one row, and purling the next. This pattern is repeated to the end of the knitting. For stockinette stitch, the right side is the knit side. For reverse stockinette stitch, the right side is the purl side.

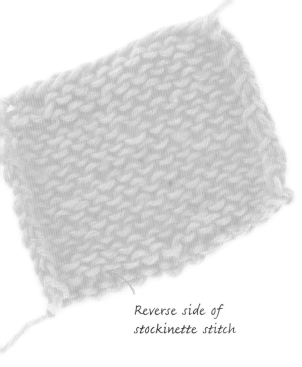

*Reverse side of
stockinette stitch*

ROUGH AND SMOOTH

A myriad of patterns can be made just with combinations of these two stitches. Other stitch patterns that are required for the projects are found throughout the book.

TIP

✳ Experiment with knit and purl stitches creating different textures. When changing from one stitch to the other, be sure to have your yarn behind for knit, and in front for purl rows.

BASKETWEAVE

This pattern looks complicated, but it is really just a clever combination of knit and purl stitches. For this version on a multiple of 6 stitches, knit 3 then purl 3 for 3 rows, then change to purl 3, knit 3 for 3 rows. Keep changing every 3 rows to create the squares. The poncho design uses another version of this pattern—4 stitches x 3 rows. (See page 82 for instructions).

Basketweave stitch

Rib Stitches

Vertical combinations of knit and purl are called ribs. They have great elasticity, useful for cuffs and necklines. Ribs can be as big as you want. This book only contains instructions for up to 3 stitches but experiment with huge ribs and bulky yarns.

SEEING STARS

✳ When the pattern includes an asterisk like this * it means that you should repeat the steps inside the two asterisks only—not other information that may come before and after.

SINGLE RIB
1 x 1 rib knitted on an even number of stitches
Step 1
On the first row knit 1, purl 1 and repeat to the end.
Step 2
Starting with the knit 1 again, repeat this same pattern for all rows.

1 x 1 rib on an odd number of stitches
Alternate rows start on a knit or a purl.
Step 1
On the first row knit 1, *purl 1, knit 1; repeat from * to the end.
Step 2
On the second row purl 1, * knit 1, purl 1; repeat from * to the end.
Step 3
Repeat steps 1 and 2.

TRIPLE RIB

3 x 3 rib knitted on multiples of 6 stitches

Step 1

On the first row knit 3, purl 3, and repeat to the end.

Step 2

Repeat this pattern for all rows.

On multiples of 6 (plus 3 extra stitches)

Step 1

On the first row knit 3, *purl 3, knit 3; repeat from * to the end.

Step 2

On the second row purl 3, * knit 3, purl 3; repeat from * to the end.

Step 3

Repeat steps 1 and 2.

DOUBLE RIB

2 x 2 rib knitted on multiples of 4 stitches

Step 1

On the first row knit 2, purl 2, and repeat to the end.

Step 2

Repeat this pattern for all rows.

On multiples of 4 (plus 2 extra stitches)

Step 1

On the first row knit 2, *purl 2, knit 2; repeat from * to the end.

Step 2

On the second row purl 2, * knit 2, purl 2; repeat from * to the end.

Step 3

Repeat steps 1 and 2.

Eyelets

This stitch looks fancy but is really easy once you understand it. Yarn-overs are used as the basis for most lacy knitting.

The yarn-overs create the picot edging on these petals.

FANCY MOVES

The yarn-over method is used in this book to make the Knitted Corsage project (page 128).

To make a small hole, or eyelet, take the yarn to the front between the needles, then over the right hand needle without knitting it, and knit the next two stitches together as one. On the following row, knit the yarn over the needle as a normal stitch, and there will be a hole beneath it while maintaining the same number of stitches in the row. Eyelets are also useful for threading ribbons through as a decorative effect.

ON A KNIT ROW

Pass the yarn under the point of the right needle (to front), then over the needle to the back again. Then knit the next two stitches together.

ON A PURL ROW

Pass the yarn up over the right needle and to the back, then around and under the point of the needle to the front again. Then purl the next two stitches together.

On a purl row take the yarn over the front of the needle

Gauge Swatches

It is hard to stress how important gauge is to the success of your finished knitting. Swatches are also a great way to practice.

SIZE MATTERS

The basis of any knitting design is called tension or gauge—the number of stitches and rows that will fit into a given size. It is very important—if it is ignored it may lead to garments that are too large or too small.

MAKE A SWATCH

Before you start any project you need to make a gauge square (at least 4 inches x 4 inches) and then measure it with a tape measure. This will enable you to work out the number of stitches per inch and therefore the number of stitches you will need to cast on, and the number of rows you will need to work.

Thin needles will make more stitches per inch than fat ones.

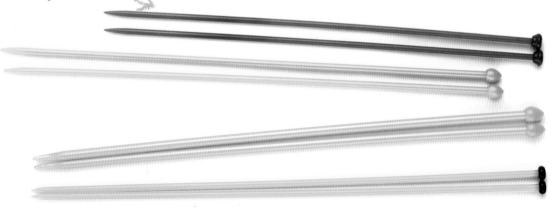

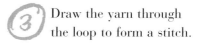

✳ To tie a slipknot—make a loose loop and pull a second loop through the center of the first loop, adjusting the tail end to secure.

❋ If you are binding off the neckline of a garment, such as the neck of a child's sweater, you don't want it to be too tight, so make sure you bind-off loosely here.

Measure the
number of rows
and stitches
every 4 inches.

INDIVIDUAL TENSION

Even if you are using the same weight yarn
as used in the projects, you may find your
tension differs from the pattern. You can
get closer to the pattern's gauge by using
smaller needles if you are a loose knitter, or
larger ones if you have too many stitches
per inch. But if you alter yarn thickness,
you may have to adapt the design
accordingly using a gauge swatch as a guide

Yarns will have
more or less
stitches per
inch, depending
on the thickness.

Odds and Ends

Weave in any loose ends using a blunt-ended needle, working through the seams, or the back of the stitches—knots will only work loose.

Use a blunt-ended needle and the same color yarn as the knitting. Place the two sides to be joined side by side. Match the stitches, row by row, all the way up to the top. Insert the needle under two strands, between the first stitch and the second. The needle then goes back in at the same place that it came out.

Mattress stitch is nearly invisible

Backstitch is hardwearing

Place the right sides together, making sure the edges are even with each other. Using the same yarn that you knitted in and a blunt needle, make a long stitch forward and a short stitch back. Keep a straight row, one stitch in from the edge.

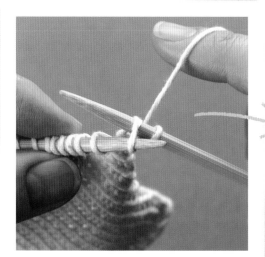

Increasing a stitch by knitting into the back

Knit the first stitch, but instead of dropping the stitch off the left needle, place the point of the right needle into the back of the stitch, knit it and then drop it off the left needle. To decrease just knit 2 stitches together.

To decrease the number of stitches, knit two together

Joining a new ball of yarn

Unless you are desperately short of yarn, always join a new ball at the end of a row. Simply stop knitting with one strand, and pick up the new one. Leave a 6–8 inch tail, loop the ends loosely and weave them into the seam later on. If you are planning stripes, make them an even number of rows. Run the second color loosely along the edge.

Dropped Stitches

However careful you are, there will always be an occasion when something goes wrong. Some mistakes, like a dropped stitch, can be easily remedied and are worth taking the time to fix.

1 With the stitch at the front of your work, use a knitting needle to pick up the horizontal threads, pulling each thread through the stitch one at a time.

2 When you have picked up all the dropped stitches, place the stitches back on your needle.

TIP

✳ All the stitches should be facing the same way in a row for neatness. If you are winding the yarn around the needle in a clockwise direction (see page 24) the stitches should all face to the left, so return your dropped stitches back on the needle facing left.

③ You may find it easier where there is a long ladder, to use a crochet hook. Insert the hook through the dropped stitch from front to back. Catch the lowest strand on the hook before pulling it through the stitch.

④ Repeat until all the strands have been used. Work your way across the row and place the new stitch back on the needle.

Customizing:
Do your own thing

This book includes a wide variety of ideas, but none of them is set in stone—the patterns can be adapted to suit your style.

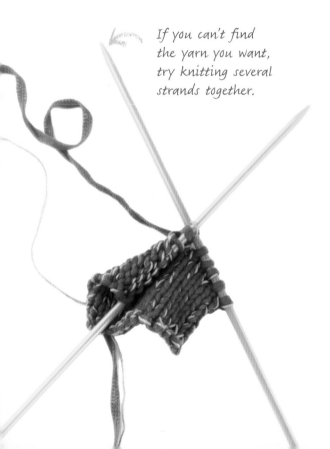

If you can't find the yarn you want, try knitting several strands together.

SPRINGBOARD

Use the patterns in this book as a basis from which you can create complex and individual designs of your own. Whether this involves changing the color of the yarn, the needle size, type of yarn, or the finishing touches—be as daringly original as you can! Scavenge thrift stores for quirky woolen pieces that can either be customized by cutting and stitching, or unravelled to make full use of the yarn. Recycle old fabric by cutting it into thin strips and knitting it into a new design. Try not to limit yourself to traditional textile materials—you can knit plastic bags, strips of paper, lengths of string, packaging tape—anything that comes in a long length, or that can be tied together, is fair game.

*Decorate your life
with flowers and daisies.*

BE UNIQUE

New crafters should strive to be original—
trawl markets or the Internet for vintage
yarns and patterns. Create your own
unique, individual clothes and accessories
instead of copying mass-market knitwear.

This book will encourage you to have
fun inventing designs of your own.
Remember, there are no set rules.
Anything goes in fashion!

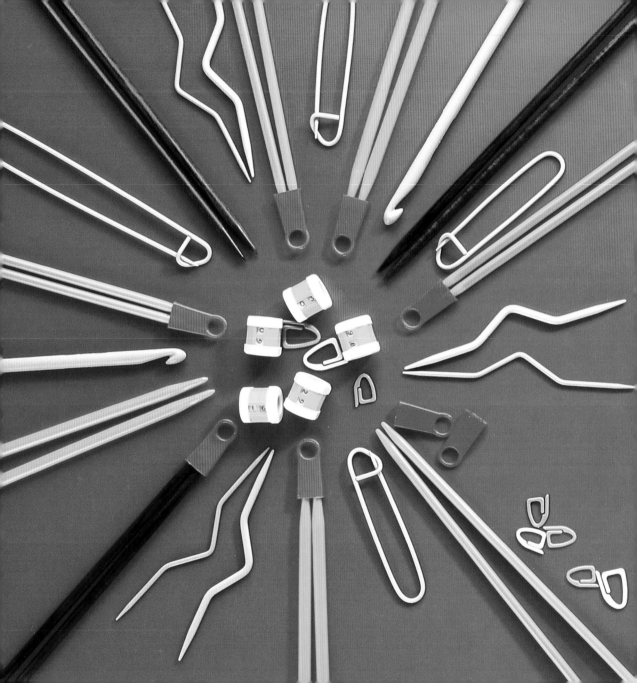

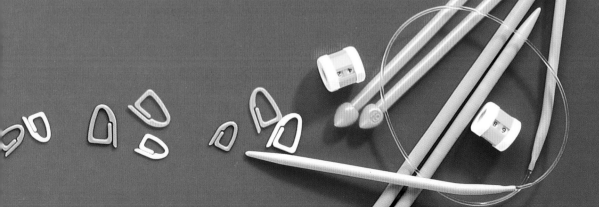

Knitting
Projects

Knobbly, Bobbly *Belt*

This belt can be worn either knotted around your hips or as a *crazy scarf.* The dangling OVAL BALLS are like pine cones and are a real conversation starter.

The basic belt is made up of simple garter stitch.

YOU WILL NEED

Needles: #6/4mm

Yarn: 3½ ounces double knitting yarn

Gauge: 11 stitches and 22 rows = 2 inches

Stitch Type: Garter stitch

How to make
the *Belt*

Dangly pine cones
could be replaced
with pom-poms.

*Use two balls of yarn so
that the fabric is stronger.*

(1) Cast on 12 stitches using
two strands of the same-
colored yarn as if it were one.

(2) Knit every row until the belt reaches
about 47 inches. Bind off and weave
in the ends (see page 38).

Make the Balls

Toy stuffing is ideal, but you can use scraps of yarn.

2 Gather by running stitches across the top and bottom of the rectangle. Before you close up the ball, stuff with toy stuffing. Stitch up and pull tight to secure. Leave a 12-inch tail. Repeat until you have 9 balls in color one. Knit 1 ball in color two. Knit 2 balls with a stripe.

The pattern for the striped balls is:

4 rows color one; 4 rows color two;

2 rows color one; 4 rows color two;

4 rows color one.

Attach the balls to the belt by stitching 3 to one end and 9 to the other end.

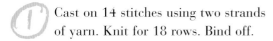

1 Cast on 14 stitches using two strands of yarn. Knit for 18 rows. Bind off.

Cozy Cowl

This cowl is so *snug and versatile*. Pull it right up over your HEAD to keep warm on a cold day, or roll it down around your neck.

Chunky 3 x 3 rib.

Garter stitch buttons.

YOU WILL NEED

Needles: #15/10mm

Yarn: 14 ounces bulky yarn
3½ ounces bulky yarn for the big pom-pom
1¾ ounces double knit yarn for the small pom-pom

Gauge: 7 stitches and 10 rows = 4 inches

Stitch Type: 3 x 3 Rib

Other Equipment: Pom-pom templates

How to make
a Cozy *Cowl*

Make the pom-poms
in any color you like
(see page 100)

 Cast on 54 stitches. Knit 3,
purl 3, and repeat to the end of
the row. Repeat this for 42 rows.

2 Bind off loosely, keeping to the rib
pattern in the last row.

When sewing up ribs take in
½ stitch, rather than a whole one.

3 Stitch up the sides to make a
tube using mattress stitch.
Weave in the ends (see page 38).

4 Make 2 pom-poms, 1 large
one, and 1 medium one.
Stitch them to the side of the cowl
about 1 inch up from the bottom.
Knit covered buttons (see page
136) and attach to the cowl.
Weave the ends into the seam
(see page 38).

Headband and *Cuffs*

2 x 2 rib

This *stretchy* headband, with matching cuffs, is a real SHOWSTOPPER. Customize them with clusters of bright pom-poms, badges, or buttons.

The blue pom-poms here have been through the wash to make them soft, like felt.

YOU WILL NEED

Needles: #10/6mm

Yarn: 3 ½ ounces bulky yarn
Various bulky yarns for the pom-poms

Gauge: 14 stitches and
19 rows = 4 inches

Stitch Type: 2 x 2 Rib

Other Equipment: Pom-pom templates

How to make a Headband and *Cuffs*

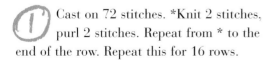 Cast on 72 stitches. *Knit 2 stitches, purl 2 stitches. Repeat from * to the end of the row. Repeat this for 16 rows.

(2) Cast off leaving a 12-inch tail—use this end to stitch up the sides.

 Weave in the ends (see page 38). Repeat step 1 with 32 stitches to make the cuff.

Now make 7 pom-poms—1 medium pink pom-pom, 3 medium yellow pom-poms, and 3 small blue pom-poms. Put the 3 blue pom-poms in the washing machine to achieve the felted effect in the picture. It's fine to put them in with the household wash, just make sure they are with similar colored items so you don't get any unexpected results. Stitch on the pom-poms anyway you like.

Zippy *Purse*

Using a range of ZINGY YARNS in strong colors, make yourself this quirky purse. Be sure to use a *lively fabric* as a lining and put as many flowers on it as you want.

YOU WILL NEED

Needles: # 6/4mm

Yarn: 2 x 3 ½ ounce fingering yarn in contrasting colors

Gauge: 23 stitches and 30 rows = 4 inches

Stitch Type: Stockinette stitch

Other Equipment: Zipper—6 inches approx
Button
Lining fabric—8 x 12 inches approximately.

How to make a Zippy *Purse*

Use two strands together to get a thicker, tighter result.

① Cast on 40 stitches in color one. Knit 1 row, purl 1 row. Change to color two, knit 1 row, purl 1 row. Continue these stripes for 66 rows.

② Bind off on a knit row. Fold in half lengthwise with the right sides together and stitch up the sides.

TOP TIP

✱ We made this super zipper-pull like a knitted ball without sewing up the sides (see page 49).

(3) Make sure the zipper is closed and stitch back the two fabric ends of the zipper next to the fastener. With the purse inside out, pin the zipper to the back of one side of the purse. Using backstitch attach the zipper to the purse. Open the zipper and repeat on the other side.

To make the lining, measure the width and depth of your purse. Add ¾ inch to both measurements to allow for the seams, and double the depth. Fold the cut fabric in half depthwise and with the right sides together pin and stitch up the two sides ⅜ inch away from the edge, starting at the fold.

(4) Fold down the top raw edge by ⅜ inch and baste (see page 91). Insert the lining into the purse so both wrong sides are together. Pin it in place, leaving clearance for the zipper. Backstitch neatly in place. Add your decorations and zipper-pull if desired.

Knitted *Bag*

This bag is practical, *fun*, and just big enough for all your ESSENTIAL JUNK—even your knitting.

Knitted in 1 x 1 rib, this bag uses knit and purl stitches.

YOU WILL NEED

Needles: #10/6mm

Yarn: 7 ounces bulky yarn

Gauge: 11 stitches and 18 rows = 4 inches

Stitch Type: 1 x 1 Rib

Other Equipment: 2 wooden handles
Lining fabric—10 x 24 inches
approximately

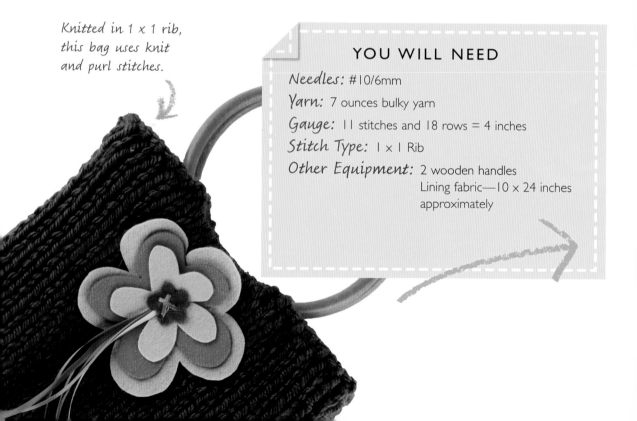

How to make
a Knitted *Bag*

1 Cast on 44 stitches. Knit 1, purl 1, and repeat to the end of the row. Repeat this pattern for 90 rows. Bind off. Fold in half lengthwise with the right sides together and stitch up the sides. Darn in the ends (see page 38).

2 To make the lining, measure the width and depth of your purse. Add ¾ inch to both measurements to allow extra material for the seams. Don't forget to double the depth measurement. Cut your fabric to the required size. Fold your fabric in half depth-wise and with the right sides together pin down the sides. With small backstitches, stitch up the two sides ⅜ inch away from the edge, starting at the fold.

3 Fold down the top raw edge to the wrong side by 1 inch and baste all the way around.

4 Insert the lining into the bag so that both wrong sides are together. Pin and blanket stitch neatly in place (see page 95). Attach the handles by stitching a small folded over section on each side. Attach your chosen decoration on each side, just below the handles. We used a felt flower (see page 122).

Big Scarf

 COZY AND CUTE, this scarf knits up quickly. Wear it like a shawl or *wrapped casually* around your neck, depending on your mood.

This scarf looks lacy and complicated, but is actually really easy to knit!

YOU WILL NEED

Needles: #19/15mm

Yarn: 3 ½ ounce ball bulky chenille yarn

Gauge: 3 stitches and 2 rows
= approximately 4 inches

Stitch Type: Elongated stitch

How to make a Big *Scarf*

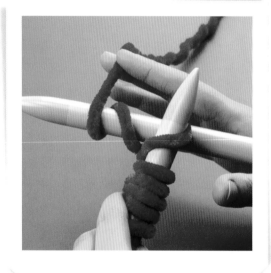

Cast on 14 stitches. Knit as normal but on each stitch, wrap the yarn around twice before slipping the stitch off the left needle. Knit the whole row in this way.

Knit into only one wrap on the following row and let the other wrap drop off the needle.

3 Repeat these two rows 15 times or until the scarf is the length that you want.

4 Bind off. Gather the ends with a running stitch and add a ball or pom-pom. Darn in the loose ends (see page 38).

Big knitted balls add color (see page 106).

Bobble *Hat*

Beat the blizzard with this bobble hat! It is knitted in a lovely blackberry stitch and is made extra special by its finishing touches—CORKSCREWS and a big *fluffy pom-pom.*

This simple hat is just a square gathered together at the top.

YOU WILL NEED

Needles: #10/6mm

Yarn: 7 ounces bulky yarn
1 ¾ ounces bulky yarn for the pom-pom
1 ¾ ounces double knitting yarn for the spool knitted tie

Gauge: 16 stitches and 9 rows = 4 inches

Stitch Type: Blackberry stitch

Other Equipment: Pom-pom templates
Spool bobbin

How to make a Bobble *Hat*

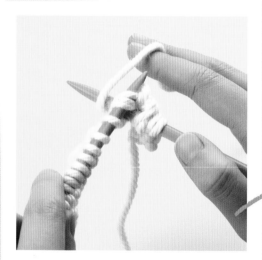

Put the needle through 3 stitches at once, and knit to make 1

1. Cast on 76 stitches and knit one row. On the second row, decrease by knitting 3 stitches together (see page 39).

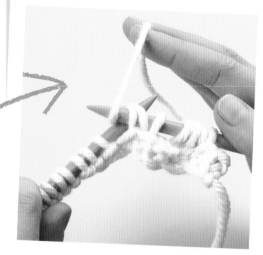

Work 1 stitch 3 times to increase.

TOP TIP

✳ Make 1 medium pom-pom (see page 100) and 3 corkscrews (see page 148), stitching them to the hat near the pull cord.

2. Next, increase—purl 1, knit 1, purl 1—into the next stitch. Repeat this to the end of the row. The surface will become bobbly as you progress.

3 Knit the next row. Repeat this pattern, with one bobbly row and one plain row, until you have knitted 40 rows. Bind off. Stitch up the sides to make a tube. Darn in the ends (see page 38).

fluffy pom-poms will add color

4 Spool knit (see page 142) 16 inches of cord using a contrasting colored yarn. Thread it in and out of the knitting about 2 inches from the top, pull tight, and knot.

Loopy *Scarf*

This scarf LOOKS DIFFICULT but is well worth the

effort. Persevere with juggling the ruler and I promise the

outcome will be *fantastic*.

The furry finish is made with a ruler!

YOU WILL NEED

Needles: #10/6mm

Yarn: Work three strands of yarn together
3 ½ ounces double knitting yarn
3 ½ ounces fingering thin cotton
1 ¾ ounces fine mohair

Gauge: 13 stitches and 10 rows = 4 inches
(measured on reverse side)

Stitch Type: Fur stitch

Other Equipment: Long ruler

How to make a Loopy *Scarf*

① Using three strands together as one, cast on 18 stitches. Knit one row. On the second row, insert the needle into the stitch, then wrap the yarn first around the needle, then around the ruler (held behind the needle), then again around the needle. Keep the wraps very loose to make things easier for yourself later on!

knit from front to back, as usual, but with both wraps

② Draw the two wraps on the right needle through the stitch on the left needle and drop this stitch from the needle. Repeat this for each stitch across the row.

3 On the next row knit into the back of the two wraps from each loop. Keep the loops on the ruler for the whole of the row.

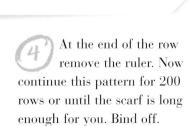

4 At the end of the row remove the ruler. Now continue this pattern for 200 rows or until the scarf is long enough for you. Bind off.

Fuzzy
Leg Warmers

Keep *warm* with these fuzzy leg warmers.

Knitwear has never looked so good!

YOU WILL NEED

Needles: #7/4.5mm

Yarn: 10 ½ ounces bulky yarn
7 ounces mohair
3 ½ ounces double knitting yarn
for the pom-poms

Gauge: 15 stitches and 13 rows = 4 inches

Stitch Type: Garter stitch and elongated stitch

Other Equipment: Pom-pom template

How to make Fuzzy *Leg Warmers*

1 Cast on 60 stitches in the bulky yarn. **Row 1 and 2** Knit 2 rows. **Row 3** Change to the mohair and knit 3 stitches. On the next stitch, *wrap the yarn around the needle twice and knit as normal. *

2 Repeat from * to * for 5 more stitches. You should now have 3 normal stitches and 6 elongated stitches on the needle. Now knit 6 stitches wrapping the yarn around once only. Repeat this pattern of 6 elongated stitches and 6 knit stitches to stitch 58 (3 stitches from the end). Knit these last three stitches normally. **Row 4** Repeat this row only knitting into the first wrap of the elongated stitches. **Row 5 and 6** Change to the thicker yarn again, and knit 2 rows normally, remembering to only knit into the first wrap of the elongated stitches. **Row 7 and 8** Change back to the mohair yarn and knit 3 elongated stitches. Now repeat the pattern from Row 3 and 4—knit 6 normal stitches and then 6 elongated stitches to stitch number 58. Elongate the last 3 stitches. Repeat this for Row 8. Repeat this 8 row pattern for 112 rows. Bind off.

(3) Stitch up the sides to make a tube. Darn in the ends (see page 38). Spool knit (see page 142) four pieces of cord 28 inches long. Make four blue, medium pompoms and two orange, medium pom-poms. Thread the length of cord in a very loose running stitch around the top and bottom of the leg warmer.

(4) Attach the blue pom-poms to both ends of the tie at the top of each legwarmer. Attach the orange pom-pom to the base of each leg warmer.

Poncho

This QUIRKY Poncho with its *massive tassels* makes a real statement! The basketweave stitch adds real texture and weight to this unusual piece.

YOU WILL NEED

Needles: #17/12.75 mm

Yarn: 21 ounces bulky yarn
7 ounces bulky yarn for tassels
1 ¾ ounces double knit yarn
for tassels

Gauge: 9 stitches and 12 rows = 4 inches

Stitch Type: Basketweave stitch

Other Equipment: Tassel template

How to make a *Poncho*

1 Cast on 52 stitches.
Row 1 *Knit 4, purl 4, repeat from * to the last 4 stitches, knit 4.
Row 2 *Purl 4, knit 4, repeat from * to the last 4 stitches, purl 4.
Row 3 and 4 Repeat rows 1 and 2.
Row 5 As row 2.

2 **Row 6** as row 1.
Row 7 and 8, repeat rows 2 and 1.
Repeat this pattern of 8 rows 18 times.

3 Bind off the finished rectangle.
Fold so that the short, bound-off edge
meets the long edge, and opposite diagonal
corners meet, leaving a space for the head. In
the diagram, A meets A, and B meets B.

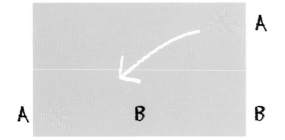

A

A   B   B

4 Join the bound-off edge to the side
using mattress stitch, and then darn
in the loose ends (see page 38).

5 Make 4 chunky tassels
and attach them along
the seam (see page 110 for
how to make tassels).

*Tassels add the
finishing touch.*

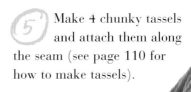

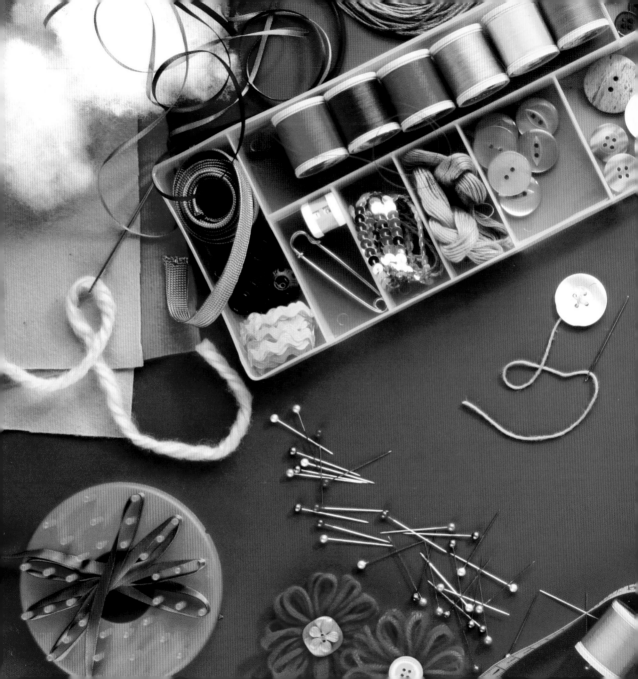

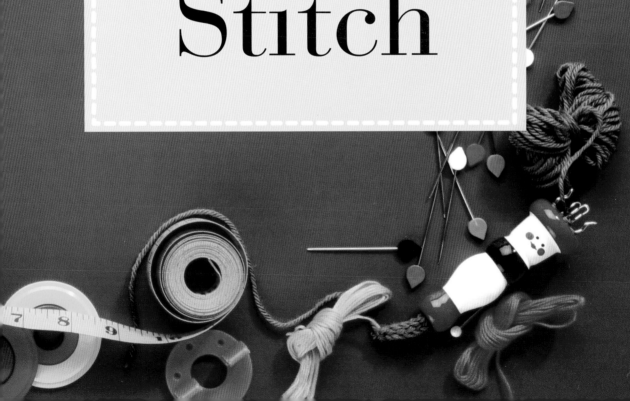

How to
Stitch

Tools for Sewing

You may already have most of the basic equipment for sewing. Start a collection of colored ribbons, threads, buttons, and beads to decorate your knitted creations.

glass-headed pins

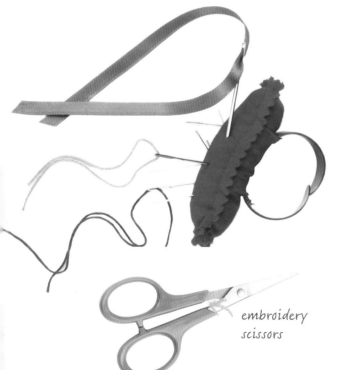

embroidery scissors

SEWING NEEDLES

You will need sewing needles to sew up your work and to decorate it. For straightforward sewing-up, use a large-eyed, blunt needle, but for some of the stitch techniques, you will need one or two sharp-ended needles in varying sizes, depending on the thickness of the thread.

SCISSORS

These don't need to be big, but they should be sharp.

TAPE MEASURE

Use a dressmaker's tape or a rigid ruler if you prefer.

embroidery
floss

ribbons

buttons

rick-rack
braid

PINS

Used for pinning together fabrics, pins
need to be sharp so they don't snag the
fabric or knitting. Glass-headed pins are
great to use as they are easy to see and
handle. Safety pins or kilt pins can be used
on the reverse of your adornments so that
they can be placed and removed easily.

colorful
threads

TOY STUFFING

This is used for the knitted balls project.
Make sure that you buy the washable
variety so that it is easier to care for
your creations.

pom-pom templates

TEMPLATES

These are plastic formers for making pom-
poms or daisy shapes. Pom-pom templates
come as simple circles or in two halves,
which are faster to make since you don't
have to thread the yarn through a hole.

lazy-daisy
maker

Basic Sewing

Stitching is essential to hold the final pieces of your creations together. There is a variety of seams depending on the nature of the garment.

BACKSTITCH

This is the most basic and secure stitch for sewing up knitted and fabric seams. If you are sewing knitting, try to use the same yarn to sew up as you have for the fabric so that it doesn't show. For fabrics, use a matching color, or contrasting one if the stitches are a decorative feature.

For this stitch, you must move two steps forward and one step back for every stitch. Place the right sides of the work together with the edges even. If you have a long seam, hold the edges together with knitting pins to ensure the seam is even along the length. Make a small stitch backward, from left to right. Then make a double length stitch forward on the wrong side. The stitches running along the right side should be small and continuous.

BASTING STITCH

This is an easy way to hold the work together temporarily while you are working. Make stitches about $\frac{1}{4}$ inch to $\frac{1}{3}$ inch long and space them well apart. If you need to unpick the stitches later they will be quicker to remove than small, tight stitches. Use a contrasting color so they will be easier to see.

RUNNING STITCH

This is similar to basting, but the stitches are closer together. It is most commonly used to gather the edges of a fabric, or to ease two differing lengths together. Take several stitches onto the point of the needle before drawing the thread through (see page 131)

Felt is easy to work with since the edges don't fray.

Embroidery

Experiment with different stitches, repeating patterns along seam edges or on the front of your piece to add that special touch.

Finishing your edges with embroidery can be very effective. These are three of the most basic embroidery stitches. Add a personal interpretation by mixing the colors and thickness of the yarns. To start, fasten your thread with a simple backstitch, and be sure to darn the ends carefully (see page 38), making sure they don't show on the right side.

CROSS-STITCH

This stitch is simple but effective. It is also known as counted thread work, since to make a square, it is necessary to count an equal number of holes in all directions. However, unlike woven cross-stitch fabrics, knitting usually has more rows than stitches per inch, so you may find that you have fewer rows than stitches in each "square."

1. Starting at one edge, take your needle from back to front. Count out an approximate square, taking the needle in at the upper right corner. Bring the needle back up in the bottom right corner and then in at the top left corner to form a cross. Bring the needle out at the start of the next stitch.

(2) Start the next cross by bringing the needle in at the diagonal corner, and completing the same process again.

A row of cross-stitches would make great decoration.

(3) Complete each cross in the same order and direction, so that all the top threads run in the same direction. To finish off, do a simple backstitch and run the thread to the edge of the work.

FRENCH KNOTS

These are great fillers for large areas of
space if repeated in a row, or raised bobbles
clustered together in a group like berries.

French knots: simple
but effective.

① Fix your embroidery thread or yarn at
the back of your work with a simple
backstitch, then bring the needle through to
the front of your work. Make a simple
overhand knot, and carefully push it down to
sit on the surface of your knitting with your
fingertips.

② Tighten the knot, and bring the
needle back in, almost at the same
spot. If you want a larger bobble, tie a second
knot in the same way before finishing off.

BLANKET STITCH

Blanket stitch can look great. To show it at its best, the edging should be done in a contrasting yarn. The size of the stitches will depend on the thickness of the yarn, and distance between the stitches.

2 Bring the thread back down and through the loop, pulling the thread firmly. Run the thread along the edge of the fabric, and then take back up to start again.

1 Working from left to right, bring the thread through to the top side of the fabric, about ½ inch from the edge. Make a loop with the thread and hold it in position with the thumb.

As its name implies, blanket stitch is good for edging blankets (and scarves, and sweaters...).

Stitching
Projects

Pom-Poms

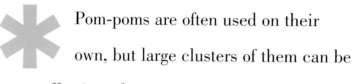

Pom-poms are often used on their own, but large clusters of them can be very effective—let your imagination run wild!

YOU WILL NEED

Yarn: chunky yarn = big pom-pom
Other Equipment: 2 pom-pom templates

You can make your own *templates* out of cardboard, or use ready-made ones like these.

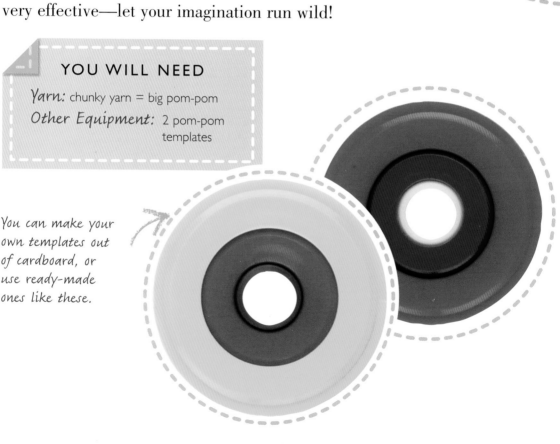

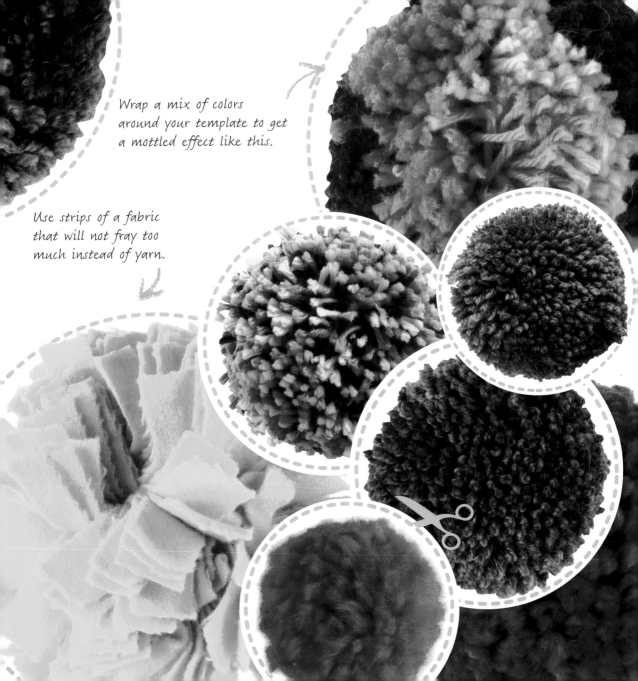

Wrap a mix of colors
around your template to get
a mottled effect like this.

Use strips of a fabric
that will not fray too
much instead of yarn.

How to make a *Pom-Pom*

Really sharp scissors will help.

2) Cut around the edge, a few layers at a time until you reach the cardboard.

1) Cut out two cardboard donuts as big as you want your pom-pom to be. Wrap the yarn around the two cards until the hole is full. You can use several strands together. Don't worry if the yarn keeps running out, just leave the ends dangling on the outside.

3 Pull the cards apart a little way, wrap the yarn around the center several times, and knot firmly. Leave the two ends long to sew the pom-pom onto your knitted piece later.

Big, bulky yarn makes a big pom-pom.

4 Remove the cards, fluff, and trim. Different effects can be achieved by altering the yarn. Wrap different colors together for a speckled effect; one after the other for stripes; and in blocks for a random effect.

How to use *Pom-Poms*

There is no end to the places that you can use pom-poms.

ALSO TRY

✳ You can make pom-poms from strips of fabric. Cut up old clothes and knot, or sew the strips together, using the lengths to make huge pom-pom variations. Felt a woollen pom-pom by washing it in hot water.

Sew a pom-pom onto a barrette or bobby pin and wear it in your hair.

Pom-poms will dress up a shopping bag.

Try pom-poms on the big, loopy scarf.

Knitted *Balls*

These balls can be made in any pattern and size. Small balls make good buttons when stuffed. The instructions are for 35 stitches and stockinette stitch. More stitches will make a fatter ball; adding more rows will make an elongated one. Experiment, and allow for plenty of yarn.

YOU WILL NEED

Needles: #10/6mm

Yarn: 2 x 3 ½ ounces bulky yarn in contrasting colors

Gauge: Not crucial

Stitch Type: Stockinette stitch

Other Equipment: Toy stuffing

Knit balls in big bulky yarn.

Stripes are easy in
even numbered rows.

The gauge doesn't
matter too much,
the balls will just
change size.

How to make a Knitted *Ball*

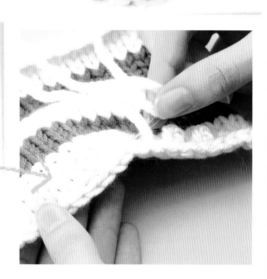

Chunky stripes

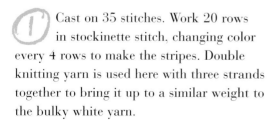

1 Cast on 35 stitches. Work 20 rows in stockinette stitch, changing color every 4 rows to make the stripes. Double knitting yarn is used here with three strands together to bring it up to a similar weight to the bulky white yarn.

2 Bind off leaving an 8-inch tail. Use the tail to gather, by running stitches across the top and bottom of the rectangle.

More stitches make a longer ball, or try using garter stitch for a textured effect.

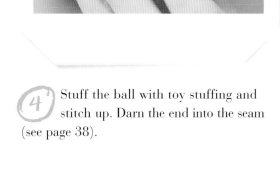

③ Pull the gathering stitches tight and secure with a small backstitch at both ends. Save the tail, as it may be long enough to sew up the seam as well.

④ Stuff the ball with toy stuffing and stitch up. Darn the end into the seam (see page 38).

How to use
Knitted *Balls*

Balls are not just for boys. Knit
yourself a set in your football
team's colors for a sporty look.

*Make a cowl with knitted
balls instead of pom-
poms, or use a
combination of both.*

ALSO TRY

✱ The gauge is not crucial, but do stuff larger balls with light toy stuffing. If you use ends of yarn, they are in danger of becoming too heavy and weighing you down.

Sew a ball onto your keys or purse, and you will never lose it again.

Tassels

Tassels are a great idea for a trim. Experiment with using multiple colors and yarns. Fine yarn will give a lovely sophisticated effect, while bulky yarn is quicker to make up—try a combination of both for texture.

YOU WILL NEED

Yarn: Bulky yarn

Other Equipment: Cardboard
Blunt needle
Sharp scissors

This tassel uses a mix of bulky cashmere and fine mohair.

Marled yarn makes
a neat tassel.

Use fine yarn, but
allow more of it.

A tail will let it swing.

How to make a *Tassel*

1 Cut a piece of cardboard 4¾ x 8 inches. Wrap the yarn loosely around the cardboard.

2 Thread a strand through the top and tie firmly leaving a short end and a long end to wind and sew later.

3 Cut the strands at the bottom with a sharp pair of scissors and trim to even up.

Using a blunt needle stops it getting from caught up between the strands.

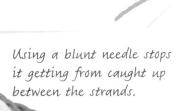

4 Hide the knot and the short end under the folded strands. Wind the long end around a few times and thread it through so that it comes out at the top. Trim ends. Use the long end to attach the tassel to your piece of knitting.

How to use *Tassels*

These chunky tassels are larger than the average tassels you may have seen before. Use the scale of them, and their number, to make a statement on any of your knitted creations.

ALSO TRY

✳ Tassels are great for tying to keys. Tie one to the backdoor key for some knitted style in your home.

Tassels make a colorful addition to the blackberry stitch hat.

In a group, the tassels have increased effect.

Wool *Daisies*

You'll be surprised at how quick and easy a daisy is to make; you can make dozens of daisies in an evening. Two daisies make a great pair of earrings, six make a wristband, and 16 make an unusual belt. It is possible to buy a daisy template, but you can make your own by simply sticking 12 ordinary pins around a circle of thick cardboard.

YOU WILL NEED

Yarn: 3 ½ ounces double knitting yarns in contrasting colors

Other Equipment:
Lazy-daisy maker or cardboard—3 ⅛ inches in diameter—and 12 pins

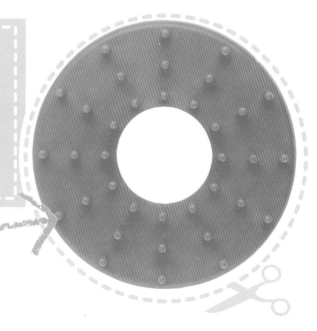

A store-bought lazy-daisy maker can make a variety of sizes.

Sew a smaller daisy
on top of a large one.

Using several colors
at once gives a
layered look.

Fine mohair
makes a
fluffy flower.

How to make a Wool *Daisy*

mentally number the spokes to make it easier.

(1) Hold the end of the yarn down with your left thumb. Working in a clockwise direction, pass the yarn with the right hand from left to right around spoke 1. Pass the yarn across the center and from left to right around spoke 2 opposite, then back across the center and from left to right around spoke 3. And so on.... Continue until all the spokes have been wrapped (once if you are using thick yarn and several times if you are using thinner yarn).

(2) Once you have finished, cut the yarn, leaving a tail of about 12 inches. Thread a needle onto the tail of the yarn. Work 13 backstitches, passing the needle under two petals and back over one.

A use for all those pretty buttons you have been saving.

(3) Make sure you do all 13 stitches or the flower won't be secure. Sew in the ends and pull out the pins to release the daisy.

(4) Attach a contrasting, pretty button as a centerpiece, or make some contrasting stitches with another yarn.

How to use Wool *Daisies*

These fantastic flowers will add a feminine touch to your knitted garments. They are smaller and lighter than some of the other decorations, and so can be used in greater numbers.

ALSO TRY

✳ Daisies will make a welcome addition to any garment. They use such a small amount of yarn, that it is a good opportunity to try out some fancy yarns, or to experiment with odds and ends from your workbox.

Cotton tape is a good yarn for daisies.

*Giant daisies give
this poncho a flower-
power appeal.*

Felt *Flowers*

These felt flowers are very quick to make and instantly perk up an outfit. These instructions are for a basic flower, but adapt it by adding embroidery, beading, or by making pointed petals.

Choose contrasting colors to go with your final project.

YOU WILL NEED

Equipment: 4 flower templates
4 contrasting colors of felt
16 inches ribbon in
    contrasting colors
Embroidery floss
Sewing thread and needle
Scissors

Make a cluster of blooms for added flower power.

How to make a Felt *Flower*

1 Copy the templates from page 156. Trace the shapes onto the felt. Cut out.

2 Lay them on top of each other, largest first, as shown. Use sewing thread to attach in the center.

These stitches will be covered up by the smallest shape.

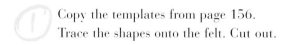

3 Cut the ribbons to various lengths, making sure you cut the ends at an angle so they don't fray. Fold the ribbons in half, and attach them to the center of the felt pieces with a basting stitch.

Choose fine, satin ribbons that complement the color and texture of the felt.

4 Place the final felt piece over the ribbons in the center of the flower. Make a large cross-stitch (see page 92). Secure at the back. Your flower is now ready to stitch onto anything you want. You could attach a safety pin to the reverse so that it can be pinned onto a coat or bag.

How to use Felt *Flowers*

A single flower will make a beautiful pin, or boutonniere for a man. Make coordinated flowers and use them to decorate napkin rings, tables, as well as people.

ALSO TRY

❋ Felt is easy to use since it doesn't fray, but don't restrict yourself to one type of fabric. Use whatever scraps you have, from flowery upholstery cloth, to wool suiting, and deliberately fray the edges.

Use felt flowers to decorate the big scarf.

Group several
flowers together on
a headband or hat.

Knitted
Corsage

Create your own cute, wool jewelry by knitting these fantastic flowers. Pin them onto coats, bags, scarves, and skirts—the possibilities are endless!

YOU WILL NEED

Needles: #6/4mm

Yarn: 2 x 1¾ ounce balls double knitting yarn in contrasting colors

Gauge: Not crucial

Stitch Type: Stockinette stitch and picot hem

Other Equipment: 2 safety pins
2 buttons

Dig out those odd buttons from your sewing box.

The contrasting
colored edge shows up
the picot shaping.

How to make a
Knitted *Corsage*

Purl the yarn-overs as if they were regular stitches.

① Cast on 55 stitches. Stockinette stitch for 10 rows, ending on a purl row. Change to the contrasting color and on the next row *Knit one, Bring the yarn forward (as if to purl) and over the needle and then knit two stitches together. Repeat from * to the end.(See page 34 for yarn over technique.)

② Return to the original color and purl the next row. Work another 10 rows of stockinette stitch.

Make a group of
corsages to liven
up a coat or bag.

3 Bind off. Darn in ends (see page 38) and trim. Fold at the eyelets with the wrong sides together and stitch along the bottom. Do this stitching with a running stitch so it can be gathered, pulled tight, and secured with a small backstitch.

4 Coil the strip around and stitch in place. Attach a contrasting button as a centerpiece and stitch a large safety pin on the reverse of the flower.

How to use
Knitted *Corsages*

These beautiful flowers are easier to make than you might think, once you get the hang of them. Ring the changes by using different colors.

ALSO TRY

These knitted roses make a great decoration on their own. Sew one to a pin, and wear it on your favorite winter coat, sweater, or bag.

This girl has come up smelling like roses.

A garden of roses
adorns this poncho.

Covered
Buttons

 You can knit all kinds of interesting buttons

with your leftover scraps of yarn.

Bulky wool will make
a chunky button.

YOU WILL NEED

Needles: #6/4mm

Yarn: Scraps of fingering yarn

Stitch Type: Garter stitch

Other Equipment: Circle of thick cardboard—
2¼ inches in diameter

Work two colors together for a stripy effect.

Decorate your buttons with more buttons or beads.

How to make a Covered *Button*

Stripes are simple and effective.

There are several approaches to making knitted buttons.

❋ Buy a button covering kit, and cover with a stretched knitted square. Unless the knitting is very fine, the back plate will not snap on. Work a running stitch around the edge with the cast-off tail. Pull tight and secure with a few stitches.

❋ Use old buttons or circles of thick cardboard to gather the knitting around.

Use old buttons to dress up your new ones!

1 Cast-on 18 stitches. Knit 2 rows in one color. Change colors as and when you want. Try alternating the color every 2 rows. Bind off. Cut a thick piece of cardboard into a 2¼ inch circle.

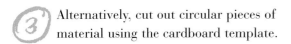

②　Using running stitch, stitch all the way around the edges and pull tight around the circle of cardboard.

③　Alternatively, cut out circular pieces of material using the cardboard template.

④　Using running stitch, stitch all the way around the edges and pull tight around the metal disk from your button covering kit.

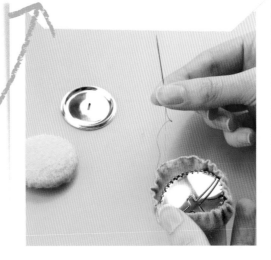

How to use
Covered *Buttons*

Don't be restricted by conventional uses of a
button, but think of these more as medallions.

*Group buttons together
to add pizzazz to this
headband.*

One single and huge
button makes a
modern looking bag.

Spool
Knitting

Spool knitting is a great way to make cords that have many applications: belts, ties, or loops for buttonholes. It is essential to allow plenty of yarn as cords often take up tremendous amounts. Use as many strands together as you like, experimenting with color and texture. If you don't have a spool you can make one with an old-fashioned wooden thread spool and four nails, making sure the top of the nails are smooth.

YOU WILL NEED

Yarn: Any fine or medium weight yarn

Other Equipment:
Knitting spool

Once you have the knack, you can make yards of cord.

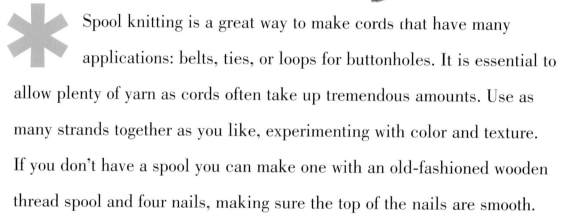

Add buttons on
top of buttons to
make a pin.

Sew buttons on with
bulky yarn and
embroidery floss.

How to make a
Spool *Knitted cord*

1 Pass your yarn all the way through your spool from head to toe.

2 To cast on, start with a slip knot (see page 17) on the first pin. Moving clockwise from one pin to another, wrap the yarn around the pin twice in a counter-clockwise direction. Using a sharp pointed stick or knitting needle, pick up the lower stitch and pass it over the top of the pin.

In the U.K. this is called corking or French knitting.

③ For the following rows you need only wrap the pin once, passing the existing stitch over the new wrap. Keep going around in the same direction. As you complete more rows, cord will start to appear at the bottom of your spool with the twisted stitches as seen in the pictures here.

TOP TIP

✱ For a speedy technique, just wrap the yarn around all the pins at once. The stitches will be untwisted and it will be less time consuming.

④ Continue until you reach the desired length. To cast off, thread the yarn on a large needle and pick up each stitch, pulling them off the pins, and drawing it tight. The resulting cord can then be coiled and stitched to create a decorative brooch.

How to use
Spool *Knitting*

Once you have the hang of spool knitting, you will make it faster than you can find things to do with it, so here are some ideas.

Group several spirals together for effect.

ALSO TRY

✳ Using several strands at once will make the cord grow more quickly, but it can be tricky. Try using a tapestry needle to pull the yarns over the hooks.

Decorated with buttons, this spiral is a singular example.

Wiggly *Corkscrews*

Corkscrews make fantastic trims. Make a basketful and sew them in a row on the end of a scarf, or the bottom of a bag, as a quirky fringe instead of tassels. Experiment with different sizes, yarns, and gauges for crazy results!

These are traditionally called wiggle-woggles.

YOU WILL NEED

Needles: #10/6mm

Yarn: Scraps of yarn

Gauge: Not crucial

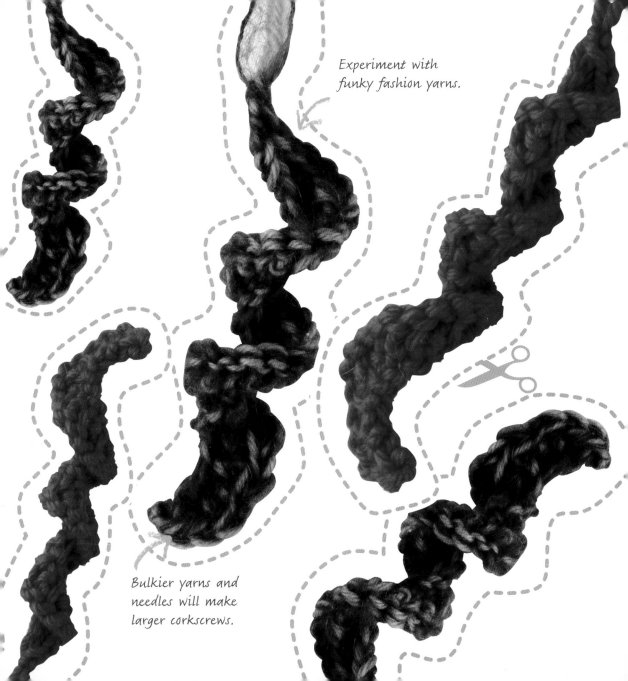

Experiment with
funky fashion yarns.

Bulkier yarns and
needles will make
larger corkscrews.

How to make a
Wiggly Corkscrew

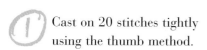 Cast on 20 stitches tightly using the thumb method.

 Now you need to double increase. This is done by knitting, and then purling, into the same stitch before slipping it off the needle. Knit the stitch as normal, and before taking the stitch off the needle, bring the yarn forward between the needles and purl the same stitch, then drop it off the needle.

3 Repeat this to the end of the row. You should now have twice as many stitches.

Experiment with increasing on the next row as well

4 Bind off very loosely— this will create a curly corkscrew shape.It is the tight edge and the increases that make the yarn curl.

How to use
Wiggly *Corkscrews*

Just use your imagination when it comes to using these. A row of corkscrews would make lovely tassels for a scarf or poncho.

Leg warmers adorned with corkscrews are de rigeur.

ALSO TRY

✳ The more stitches you start off with, the longer your corkscrews will be. The more rows that you knit, the fatter they will be. Experiment with different yarns to find the best result.

Make giant corkscrews by increasing the number of stitches in the first row.

Yarns Used for Projects

We used certain brands of yarn for the projects in the book. You can probably get hold of similar yarns, but if trying different ones do use that all important gauge swatch (see page 36).

LOOPY SCARF
ROWAN 4 Ply Soft Wool – *Shade Beetroot*
ROWAN 4 Ply Cotton – *Shade 133*
ROWAN Kidsilk Haze – *Shade 606*

HEADBAND
ROWAN Big Wool – *Shade 21*
ROWAN Biggy Print – *Shade 237*
SIRDAR Nova – *Shade 906*
DEBBIE BLISS Merino DK – *Shade 225201*

BEANIE
DEBBIE BLISS Cashmerino Super Chunky – *Shade 01, white*
ROWAN Biggy Print – *Shade 237*
DEBBIE BLISS Merino DK – *Shade 225201*

COWL
ROWAN Biggy Print – *Shade 237*
ROWAN Biggy Print – *Shade 258*
DEBBIE BLISS Merino DK – *Shade 225701*

LEG WARMERS	DEBBIE BLISS Alpaca Silk Green – *Shade 25007* ROWAN Kidsilk Haze – *Shade 597* ROWAN Kidsilk Haze – *Shade 581* DEBBIE BLISS Merino DK – *Shade 225701* DEBBIE BLISS Merino DK – *Shade* ˊ
PURSE	ROWAN 4 Ply Cotton – *Shade 13* ROWAN 4 Ply Cotton – *Shade 12ˊ* ROWAN Cotton Tape – *Shade 54ˊ*
BAG	DEBBIE BLISS Cashmerino Super Chuₙ. – *Shade 16020, purple*
BIG SCARF	SIRDAR Wow – *shade 758 Raspberry Crush* DEBBIE BLISS Super Chunky – *Shade 101* DEBBIE BLISS Super Chunky – *Shade 201*
BELT	DEBBIE BLISS Merino DK – *Shade 225701* DEBBIE BLISS Merino DK – *Shade 225700* DEBBIE BLISS Merino DK – *Shade 225704*
PONCHO	ROWAN Big Wool – *Shade 29* ROWAN Biggy Print – *Shade 245*
KNITTED FLOWERS	DEBBIE BLISS Merino DK – *Shade 225201* DEBBIE BLISS Merino DK – *Shade 225700*
YARN DAISIES	ROWAN Cotton Tape – *Shade 549*

Needle Conversions

In an ideal world we would have a standardized system for measurements and knitting needle size. Use the tables below to help you make conversions.

In Europe, the metric system is mostly used. This has the advantage that it is a direct measurement of the width of the needle. The old U.K. system, and the U.S. version use random numbers, so whenever possible, rely on the millimeter sizing. The best way to solve any problems with identifying old, or unmarked needles, is to keep a needle gauge in your knitting bag. That way you will be able to convert patterns with ease.

Always keep a needle gauge close by to help you make quick conversions.

mm	U.S./Can #	Old UK/Can Sizes
2	0	14
2.25	1	13
2.75	2	12
3		11
3.25	3	10
3.5	4	
3.75	5	9
4	6	8
4.5	7	7
5	8	6
5.5	9	5
6	10	4
6.5	10.5	3
7		2
7.5		1
8	11	0
9	13	00
10	15	000

Suppliers

Debbie Bliss and Sirdar yarns are available at:

Knitting Fever Inc
315 Bayview Avenue
Amityville, New York 11701
USA
Tel: 631-546-3600
Fax: 631-546-6871
www.knittingfever.com
Check the internet to find a store near you.

Rowan Yarns available at:

Rowan USA
Westminster Fibers
4 Townsend West
Unit 8
Nashua, NH 03063
USA
Tel: 800-445-9276
Fax: 603-886-1056
www.rowan.com

Pony needles available at:
www.ponyneedles.com
www.ponyuk.com
UK distributors: www.groves-banks.com

Author's Acknowledgments:
I would like to thank all my family for their support, especially Abigail for her assistance on the pom-pom front!

Templates

Felt flower templates

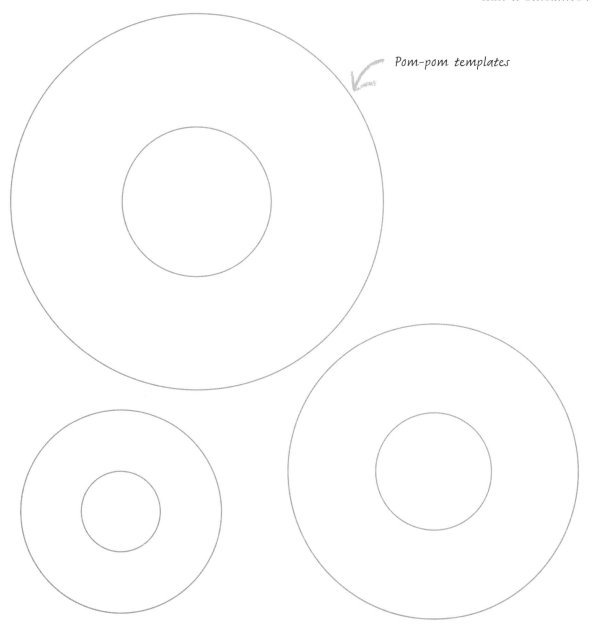

Pom-pom templates

Index